JUDGMENTS DECODED FOR DAILY PRACTICE
Your Roadmap to Legal Success

NARAYANA SWAMY .R

Advocate, **H**igh **C**ourt **of K**arnataka

Copyright © 2024 All rights reserved.

No part of this publication may be reproduced, stored in a retrieval system, or transmitted in any form or by any means electronic, mechanical, photocopying, recording, or otherwise without the prior written permission of the publisher.

ACKNOWLEDGEMENT AND DEDICATION

This book is lovingly dedicated to the memories and unwavering support of my family, who have been my greatest sources of strength and inspiration.

To my late father, **Rangappa M.K.**, and my mother, **Lakshminarasamma** your values and guidance have been the foundation of my life and work. This book is a tribute to the resilience, wisdom, and integrity you instilled in me.

To my brother, **Shivashankara** thank you for always standing by my side, offering encouragement and support in countless ways. Your belief in me has meant more than words can express.

And to my beloved wife, **Gowthami M.N** your patience, love, and encouragement have been my anchor through every step of this journey. This book would not have been possible without your strength and unwavering support.

With heartfelt gratitude, I dedicate this work to each of you.

DISCOVER MORE BOOKS BY NARAYANASWAMY.R

Simplifying the Law. Empowering Readers.

Hello, dear reader!

I'm **Narayanaswamy.R**, a practicing advocate and author passionate about making the law **accessible, practical, and easy to understand** for everyone from students and professionals to everyday citizens.

If you're reading this, you likely want to go deeper. The good news? There's **a world of legal knowledge waiting for you.**

My Most Popular Books:

  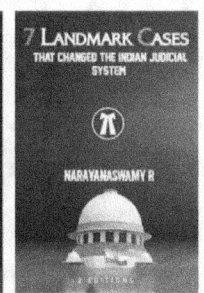

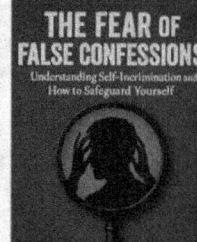

 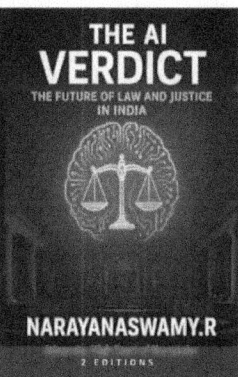 

Each book is designed with **clarity, practical insight, and real-world legal experience**.

Scan & Explore All My Books Instantly

Scan this QR code to visit my official Amazon Author Page Or click here:
https://www.amazon.com/stores/NARAYANASWAMY-R/author/B0DK4MQ6Q6?ref=ap_rdr&isDramIntegrated=true&shoppingPortalEnabled=true&ccs_id=107d9d0a-ac1d-41b4-8d9d-d8a4cb319cc2

One click can take you to your next breakthrough in understanding the law!

Preface

Welcome to "Judgments Decoded for Daily Practice." This book is **designed to help** you understand complex legal issues in **a simple manner.** Whether you're a practicing lawyer, a student aspiring to become a judge, or an experienced judge, this book has something valuable to offer.

We've also made it easy for you to access important citations. Each case includes a **QR-Code** for direct download, streamlining your legal research process.

I hope this book serves as a valuable resource on your journey through the world of law. Let's explore together and strive for excellence in legal practice and adjudication.

NARAYANASWAMY.R

Advocate **& A**uthor

WHY SHOULD YOU READ THIS BOOK??

The complexity of legal judgments, especially those delivered by various High Courts and the Supreme Court of India, often poses a challenge to legal practitioners, students, and even common citizens. As an advocate, I have frequently observed the struggle to grasp the underlying legal principles and reasoning behind these judgments. The intricate legal language, combined with the deep analytical approach adopted by the judiciary, can create hurdles not just for practicing advocates but also for judicial aspirants, law students, judges, and laypersons seeking to understand the nuances of the law.

This book, "Judgments Decoded for Daily Practice" Simplifying Legal Concepts for Advocates, Aspirants, and Laymen," is a humble attempt to bridge this gap. The idea behind this work is simple yet impactful: to take complex legal issues decided over time by the High Courts and the Supreme Court and present them in a manner that is easy to understand, without losing the essence of the law. Each case discussed in this book has been carefully selected, and the legal principles they embody have been distilled into simple, clear explanations. My goal is to make the reasoning behind each judgment accessible, while still retaining the academic rigor that practicing advocates, judicial aspirants, and judges require in their daily work.

This book is not just for legal professionals. It is designed to serve as a valuable tool for anyone interested in understanding the legal framework that governs our country. For practicing advocates, it offers a concise reference for daily practice. For judicial aspirants, it provides insight into key legal concepts and principles laid down by the judiciary. For judges, it offers clarity on the application of legal doctrines in deciding cases. Law students will find this book useful for their academic pursuits, while laypersons will appreciate the simplified approach to understanding the law.

In an ever-evolving legal landscape, it is crucial to stay informed and adapt to new interpretations of the law. Through this book, I hope to contribute to the continuous learning and growth of legal minds across the country. It is my sincere belief that by demystifying legal judgments, we can foster a deeper respect and understanding for the law.

I trust that this book will become a trusted companion to its readers, guiding them through the intricate corridors of Indian legal jurisprudence with clarity and simplicity.

- ✓ **Direct Access to Citations:** A unique feature of the book is its provision of direct download options for citations discussed in each judgment, facilitated by **QR-Codes accompanying every case study.** This innovative feature enables readers to access relevant legal authorities seamlessly, saving time and enhancing the efficiency of legal research.

TABLE OF CONTENTS

THE CASE OF CONTRABAND: KESARI'S ENCOUNTER WITH NDPS ACT _____ 13

COMPENSATION CLARITY: NATIONAL INSURANCE CO. LTD. VS. PRANAY SETHI _____ 17

PROMISE OF MARRIAGE: QUASHED EXPECTATIONS ____ 24

DISHONORED DEBTS: RESOLVING CHEQUE ALTERATION CONTROVERSIES _____ 30

LIBERTY IN LOVE: THE SHILPA SAILESH VS VARUN SREENIVASAN JUDGMENT _____ 34

PAPER VS. POSSESSION: WHY REVENUE RECORDS ALONE CAN'T PROVE LAND OWNERSHIP _____ 38

ARREST NOT A ROUTINE: SUPREME COURT PUTS CHECKS ON DOWRY CASES _____ 42

TRIAL BY FIRE: DOWRY DEATH AND DOUBT IN THE COURTROOM _____ 46

PRESUMPTION REJECTED: LANDMARK JUDGMENT IN DOWRY DEATH APPEAL _____ 50

THE ILLUSION OF CERTAINTY: A CASE OF UNRAVELING CONVICTIONS _____ 53

NECESSITY VS. CONVENIENCE: COURT DENIES EASEMENT CLAIM IN LAND DISPUTE _____ 58

PRESUMPTION, PROOF, AND THE PEN: A CASE OF
REBUTTABLE DOUBT _____ 63

TIME OF THE ESSENCE: COURT DENIES LAND TRANSFER
DUE TO LATE PAYMENT _____ 68

DEFINING "PIOUS PURPOSE": COURT CLARIFIES LIMITS
ON GIFTING ANCESTRAL PROPERTY _____ 74

CLEARING THE CONFUSION: SUPREME COURT
STREAMLINES MAINTENANCE PROCESS _____ 80

FORGET THE PAST, FOCUS ON FACTS: QUASHING AN FIR
BASED ON MERIT _____ 86

NO TURNING BACK: WHY AMENDING A SUIT CAN'T
CHANGE ITS NATURE _____ 92

PROCEDURAL CLARITY: PMLA AND CRPC INTERSECT____98

"VICTIM'S VOICE UPHOLDING CONVICTIONS IN THE
GANG RAPE CASE _____ 103

QUASHED! HOW SETTLEMENT ENDED THE LOAN
FRAUD SAGA_____ 109

.

.

.

.

.

******

Case-1

THE CASE OF CONTRABAND: KESARI'S ENCOUNTER WITH NDPS ACT

❖ UNION OF INDIA V/S SHIV SHANKER KESARI

➢ **Background of the Case:**

The case revolves around an appeal challenging the grant of bail by a Single Judge of the Allahabad High Court to the respondent, who was charged under various sections of the Narcotic Drugs and Psychotropic Substances Act, 1985 (NDPS Act), for allegedly being in possession of a substantial quantity of poppy straw. The prosecution alleged that approximately 400 Kg of poppy straw was seized from the respondent's possession. The initial bail plea was rejected by the Special Judge (NDPS Act), Varanasi, but the High Court granted bail on the grounds that the recovery was not solely from the accused and that the respondent had no prior criminal history.

➢ **Facts:**

1. The respondent was charged under Sections 8, 15, 27A, and 29 of the NDPS Act for possession of poppy straw.

2. The raiding party allegedly found nearly 400 Kg of poppy straw at the respondent's residence.

3. The District Judge rejected the bail plea based on Section 37 of the NDPS Act, which sets stringent conditions for bail in such cases.

4. The High Court granted bail, considering factors such as the absence of exclusive possession and the respondent's lack of criminal history.

> **Legal Issues:**

1. Whether the conditions specified in Section 37 of the NDPS Act were met for granting bail.

2. The interpretation of "reasonable grounds" as per Section 37(1)(b)(ii) of the NDPS Act.

3. The significance of exclusive possession in determining bail eligibility under the NDPS Act.

➢ **Court's Decision and Reasoning:**

The Supreme Court held that the High Court's decision to grant bail was unsustainable as it did not adequately consider the requirements of Section 37 of the NDPS Act. The Court emphasized that bail could only be granted if there were reasonable grounds to believe that the accused was not guilty and that they were not likely to commit any offense while on bail. The Court found that the High Court had not properly assessed these criteria and directed the bail application to be reconsidered, mandating the respondent's surrender to custody before the application's review.

➢ **Importance and Impact of the Judgment:**

This judgment reaffirms the stringent conditions for bail in NDPS cases as outlined in Section 37 of the Act. It underscores the importance of considering factors such as the likelihood of the accused committing further offenses while on bail. The decision sets a precedent for future bail applications under the NDPS Act, emphasizing the need for courts to meticulously evaluate the grounds for granting bail.

➢ **Practical Implications on Advocates and Judges:**

Advocates need to carefully analyze the requirements of Section 37 of the NDPS Act when presenting bail applications for their clients. Judges must meticulously assess bail pleas in NDPS cases, ensuring that the statutory conditions are met before granting bail. The judgment highlights the need for a thorough examination of evidence and legal principles in such cases.

➢ **Conclusion:**

The Supreme Court allowed the appeal, setting aside the High Court's bail order. The Court directed the bail application to be reconsidered in line with the provisions of Section 37 of the NDPS Act, emphasizing the necessity of the respondent surrendering to custody before the application's review. This decision underscores the strict criteria for bail in NDPS cases and emphasizes the importance of a comprehensive evaluation of bail applications in such matters

Scan Me to Download

Case-2

COMPENSATION CLARITY: NATIONAL INSURANCE CO. LTD. VS. PRANAY SETHI

NATIONAL INSURANCE COMPANY LIMITED VS. PRANAY SETHI

> Background of the case:

The case of National Insurance Company Limited vs. Pranay Sethi (2017 SCC OnLine SC 1270) emerged against the backdrop of a series of legal precedents and evolving jurisprudence surrounding compensation in motor accident claims in India. The foundation for determining motor accident compensation was laid down in the landmark case of Sarla Verma vs. Delhi Transport Corporation (2009) 6 SCC 121. In Sarla Verma, the Supreme Court established fundamental principles and guidelines for computing compensation in motor accident cases, emphasizing the concept of "just compensation" based on fairness, reasonableness, and equity.

However, despite the clarity provided by Sarla Verma, subsequent cases revealed discrepancies and differing interpretations in the application of compensation principles, particularly concerning future prospects for victims who were permanently employed, received fixed salaries, or were self-employed. These discrepancies led to a difference of opinion among benches of the court, notably in cases such as Reshma Kumari vs. Madan Mohan and Rajesh vs. Rajbir Singh.

As a result of these differing interpretations and opinions, the matter was referred to a constitution bench of the Supreme Court to provide comprehensive guidelines on the fixation of future prospects in motor accident cases. The objective was to ensure consistency, fairness, and uniformity in the calculation of compensation to better serve the interests of victims and their dependents.

Against this backdrop, the case of National Insurance Company Limited vs. Pranay Sethi (2017 SCC OnLine SC 1270) assumes significance as it sought to address the unresolved issues and discrepancies in the computation of motor accident compensation. The judgment rendered in this case not only clarified the application of multipliers and future prospects income but also provided a standardized method for determining compensation, thereby establishing crucial precedents for future motor accident claims cases in India.

The judgment in the case of National Insurance Company Limited vs. Pranay Sethi (2017 SCC OnLine SC 1270) considered several important points in the determination of motor accident compensation:

1. Approval of Multiplier Table: The court approved the multiplier table provided in the Sarla Verma case to remove any discrepancies in the calculation of compensation.

2. Application of Sarla Verma Guidelines: It emphasized the importance of applying Column (4) of the Table in Sarla Verma for selecting the multiplier, ensuring fairness and consistency in awards.

3. Multiplier for Victims Up to 15 Years: In cases where the victim's age is up to 15 years, a specific multiplier of 15 and assessment as indicated in the Second Schedule were to be followed.

4. Standardization of Compensation Computation: The judgment highlighted the need to move towards a standard method of selecting multipliers, determining future prospects income, and deducting personal and living expenses to ensure uniformity and fairness in compensation awards.

5. Addition to Deceased's Actual Salary: Future prospects income was to be added to the deceased's actual salary, with varying percentages based on the age of the deceased and their employment status.

6. **Reasonable Figures for Conventional Heads:** The court fixed reasonable figures for conventional heads such as loss of estate, loss of consortium, and funeral expenses, subject to enhancement every three years.

7. **Clarity on Precedents and Citations:** The judgment clarified the importance of consistency in judicial decisions and highlighted relevant precedents such as Sarla Verma vs. Delhi Transport Corporation and Reshma Kumari vs. Madan Mohan and Rajesh vs. Rajbir Singh.

8. **Practical Implications for Advocates and Judges:** The judgment provided clear guidelines for advocates and judges to follow in calculating compensation in motor accident claims, ensuring adherence to specified multipliers, future prospects income additions, and deductions for personal and living expenses.

These points collectively addressed the complexities and discrepancies in the computation of motor accident compensation, providing clarity and uniformity in the process.

> **Legal Issues Involved:**

1. Whether the multiplier specified in the Second Schedule appended to the Act should be scrupulously applied in all cases?

2. Whether the Act provides any criterion for determining the multiplicand, particularly concerning future prospects?

> **Court's Decision and Reasoning:**

1. The Court approved the table for the multiplier provided in the Sarla Verma case to remove any discrepancies.

2. It was held that applying Column (4) of the Table in Sarla Verma for selecting the multiplier ensures fairness and eliminates the likelihood of claimants receiving lesser amounts based on the section under which the claim was made.

3. In cases where the victim's age is up to 15 years, a multiplier of 15 and assessment as indicated in the Second Schedule should be followed.

4. The Court emphasized the need for a standard method of selecting the multiplier, determining future prospects income, and deducting personal and living expenses.

5. Future prospects income should be added to the deceased's actual salary, with varying percentages based on the age of the deceased and employment status.

6. Reasonable figures for conventional heads such as loss of estate, loss of consortium, and funeral expenses were fixed and subject to enhancement every three years.

> **Importance and Impact of the Judgment**

This judgment establishes clear guidelines for calculating compensation in motor accident claims, ensuring fairness and consistency in awards. It clarifies the application of multipliers and future prospects income based on the age and employment status of the deceased. By providing standard methods for computation, the judgment aims to streamline the compensation process and prevent discrepancies in awards.

➤ Relevant Precedents And Citations Used:

The judgment relies on precedents such as Sarla Verma vs. Delhi Transport Corporation for principles of motor accident compensation. It also references cases like Reshma Kumari vs. Madan Mohan and Rajesh vs. Rajbir Singh, highlighting the importance of consistency in judicial decisions.

➤ Practical Implications on Advocates and Judges:

Advocates and judges can now refer to the guidelines laid down in this judgment for calculating compensation in motor accident claims. They must ensure adherence to the specified multipliers, future prospects income additions, and deductions for personal and living expenses. This judgment provides clarity and uniformity in the determination of compensation, facilitating fair outcomes for claimants.

In conclusion, the case of National Insurance Company Limited vs. Pranay Sethi (2017 SCC OnLine SC 1270) stands as a landmark judgment in the realm of motor accident compensation in India. By addressing key issues and discrepancies in the computation of compensation, the Supreme Court provided much-needed clarity and guidance for future cases.

The judgment's approval of the multiplier table from the Sarla Verma case, along with its emphasis on applying consistent guidelines for selecting multipliers, determining future prospects income, and deducting personal and living expenses, establishes a standardized approach to compensation calculation. This standardized method aims to ensure fairness, equity, and uniformity in compensation awards, benefiting motor accident victims and their dependents.

Moreover, the clarification on precedents and citations underscores the importance of consistency in judicial decisions, enhancing legal certainty and predictability in motor accident claims cases.

In essence, the judgment in this case represents a significant step towards achieving consistency, fairness, and equity in motor accident compensation jurisprudence in India, thereby serving the interests of justice and the welfare of accident victims and their families.

Scan Me to Download

Case-3

PROMISE OF MARRIAGE: QUASHED EXPECTATIONS

SHEIKH ARIF VERSUS THE STATE OF MAHARASHTRA & ANR

➤ **Background of the Case:**

The present case involves an appeal against the registration of a First Information Report (FIR) filed against the appellant under various sections of the Indian Penal Code (IPC) and the Scheduled Castes and Scheduled Tribes (Prevention of Atrocities) Act, 1989. The appellant was accused of engaging in sexual relations with the respondent under false promises of marriage, leading to allegations of rape, criminal intimidation, and other offenses. The court, after careful consideration of the evidence and legal principles, addressed the validity of consent in such circumstances and examined the abuse of the legal process. The judgement outlines the court's findings and directives regarding the quashing of the FIR and the appellant's obligation to compensate the respondent.

➤ **Decision:**

The court allowed the appeal, quashed the FIR and subsequent proceedings, and directed the appellant to compensate the respondent. The judgement elucidates the legal principles regarding consent, false promises of marriage, and the prevention of the abuse of legal processes in criminal prosecutions.

> ➢ **Facts of the Case:**

1. Acquaintance and Relationship Establishment: The appellant and the respondent became acquainted in 2011 when the respondent was employed at a beauty parlour where the appellant attended a hair-cutting course.

2. Proposal and Alleged Consent: In June 2011, the appellant purportedly proposed a romantic relationship to the respondent, which she accepted.

3. False Promise of Marriage: The respondent alleged that the appellant engaged in sexual relations with her under the false promise of marriage, starting from 2012.

4. Pregnancy and Abortion: In February 2013, the respondent became pregnant, allegedly as a result of the relationship. The appellant accompanied her for an abortion.

5. Engagement Ceremony: Despite the alleged false promise of marriage, an engagement ceremony between the appellant and the respondent reportedly took place in July 2017.

6. Discovery of Another Engagement: The situation escalated when the respondent discovered photographs of the appellant's engagement to another woman in January 2018.

7. Filing of Complaint: Prompted by the discovery of the appellant's engagement to another woman, the respondent filed a complaint with the Sadar Police Station in Nagpur, leading to the registration of an FIR against the appellant.

> Issues:

1. Validity of Consent: The primary issue revolves around the validity of the respondent's consent in the sexual relationship with the appellant. It is to be determined whether the consent was obtained under false promises of marriage, thereby rendering it invalid.

2. Authenticity of Marriage Documentation: The authenticity and validity of the Nikahnama (Islamic marriage contract) presented by the appellant as evidence of his marriage to the respondent are also at issue. The court must ascertain whether the document is genuine and legally binding.

3. Abuse of Legal Process: Another crucial issue is whether the continuation of the criminal prosecution against the appellant constitutes an abuse of the legal process. This involves an examination of the evidence and circumstances surrounding the case to determine whether

the prosecution is justified or if it amounts to misuse of legal procedures.

> ➢ **Important Points Considered in the Judgement:**

1. The nature of the relationship between the appellant and the second respondent, including allegations of forced physical intimacy and false promises of marriage.

2. Examination of evidence, including the alleged Nikahnama (Islamic marriage contract) between the parties.

3. Determination of whether the continuation of the criminal prosecution against the appellant constitutes an abuse of the legal process.

> ➢ **Legal Issues Involved:**

1. Consent in sexual relationships and its validity in cases involving false promises of marriage.

2. Interpretation of evidence, including the validity of the Nikahnama.

3. Abuse of legal process and the court's discretion in quashing criminal proceedings.

> ➢ **Court's Decision and Reasoning:**

The court observed that while the second respondent was of legal age during the relationship, consent based on false promises of marriage is not valid. However, considering the evidence, including the Nikahnama and the second respondent's participation in engagement ceremonies, the court concluded that the physical relationship was consensual and not solely based on false promises of marriage. Hence, continuing the prosecution would be an abuse of legal process. The court directed the appellant to pay compensation to the second respondent and quashed the FIR and subsequent proceedings.

➢ Importance and Impact of the Judgement:

The judgement clarifies the legal stance on consent in sexual relationships involving false promises of marriage and underscores the importance of examining evidence thoroughly before proceeding with criminal prosecutions. It also highlights the court's role in preventing the abuse of legal processes.

➢ Relevant Precedents and Citations Used:

The court cited the case of Anurag Soni v. State of Chhattisgarh to establish the principle that consent obtained through misconception is not valid.

➢ Practical Implications on Advocates and Judges:

The judgement emphasizes the need for advocates to meticulously analyze evidence and legal precedents in cases involving allegations of sexual misconduct. It also guides judges in exercising discretion to prevent the misuse of legal procedures.

Conclusion of the Case:

The appeal was allowed, and the judgement quashed the FIR and subsequent proceedings against the appellant. The court directed the appellant to compensate the second respondent and outlined specific directives regarding the payment and investment of the compensation amount for the welfare of the child born out of the relationship.

Scan Me to Download

Case-4

DISHONORED DEBTS: RESOLVING CHEQUE ALTERATION CONTROVERSIES

H B BHAGYALAKSHMI V/S SMT CHELUVAMMA

➢ **Background of the Case:**

The appellant, a teacher, lent a sum of Rs. 2,50,000 to the respondent for her granddaughter's education and family needs. Payments were made through cheques and cash, with a promise of repayment. When the respondent issued a cheque, it bounced due to an alleged alteration. Despite legal notice, repayment was not made, leading to a complaint under Section 138 of the Negotiable Instruments Act (N.I. Act). The Trial Court acquitted the respondent, prompting this appeal.

➢ **Facts:**

- The appellant, a teacher, lent Rs. 2,50,000 to the respondent for her granddaughter's education and family needs.

- Payments were made via cheques and cash, with a promise of repayment.

- A cheque issued by the respondent bounced due to an alleged alteration, leading to a complaint under Section 138 of the N.I. Act.

> **Issues:**

- Whether the cheque alteration justified the Trial Court's acquittal.

- Whether the appellant established grounds for interference with the Trial Court's findings.

> **Important Points Considered in the Judgement:**

The appellant argued the Trial Court's acquittal was erroneous, emphasizing the absence of evidence regarding cheque alteration and the credibility of witnesses. Conversely, the respondent contended the cheque was altered, presenting a different loan amount.

> **Legal Issues Involved:**

Key legal issues revolved around the presumption of cheque issuance for debt discharge (N.I. Act Section 139), material alteration (N.I. Act Section 87), and signatory's liability for blank cheques (N.I. Act Section 20).

> **Court's Decision and Reasoning:**

The Appellate Court analyzed Sections 139, 87, and 20 of the N.I. Act. Despite apparent alteration, it noted the cheque's body wasn't materially changed, upholding the signatory's liability. The Trial Court's acquittal was overturned, and the respondent was convicted under Section 138.

> Importance and Impact of the Judgement:

This judgement clarifies legal principles concerning cheque alteration and liability, ensuring fair resolution in financial disputes. It reaffirms the significance of evidence and adherence to statutory provisions in cheque-related matters.

> Relevant Precedents and Citations Used:

The judgement referenced BASALINGAPPA v. MUDIBASAPPA (2019) 5 SCC 418, which delineated principles under Sections 118(a) and 139 of the N.I. Act, aiding in interpretation and application.

> Practical Implications on Advocates and Judges:

Advocates must diligently present evidence to establish or refute cheque alteration claims. Judges need to meticulously evaluate facts against statutory provisions and precedents to deliver equitable rulings.

➤ **Conclusion:**

The appellant's appeal was allowed, overturning the Trial Court's acquittal. The respondent was convicted under Section 138 of the N.I. Act and fined. Compensation to the appellant was ordered, with procedural directives issued for execution. The judgement ensures adherence to legal principles in cheque-related disputes, setting a precedent for future cases.

Scan Me to Download

Case-5

LIBERTY IN LOVE: THE SHILPA SAILESH VS VARUN SREENIVASAN JUDGMENT
SHILPA SAILESH VS VARUN SREENIVASAN

➢ Background of the Case:

The case of Shilpa Sailesh vs Varun Sreenivasan is a landmark in Indian family law, centered on a bitter matrimonial dispute seeking the dissolution of marriage. Shilpa Sailesh and Varun Sreenivasan, entangled in a prolonged legal battle, approached the Supreme Court for resolution. The case delves into the scope of judicial powers under Article 142(1) of the Indian Constitution, particularly concerning divorce proceedings under the Hindu Marriage Act.

➢ Facts:

Shilpa Sailesh and Varun Sreenivasan had been living apart for over six years, attempting reconciliation to no avail. Their marital strife involved various legal avenues, including domestic violence proceedings and criminal prosecutions under Section 498-A of the

Indian Penal Code. Initial legal actions under the Domestic Violence Act and Section 125 of the Criminal Procedure Code failed to resolve underlying grievances. Differing accounts and persistent disputes led to Supreme Court involvement due to lower courts' inability to provide a conclusive resolution.

> **Issues:**

1. Interpretation of Article 142(1): Whether the Court's powers under Article 142(1) allow deviation from established procedural and substantive laws.

2. Mutual Consent Divorce and Procedural Requirements: Whether the Court can dissolve a marriage by mutual consent, bypassing procedural requirements in Section 13-B of the Hindu Marriage Act.

3. Divorce in Cases of Irretrievable Breakdown: Whether the Court can grant divorce under Article 142(1) in cases of irretrievable breakdown, even if one spouse opposes.

4. Uniform Law for Divorce: Whether a uniform law recognizing irretrievable breakdown of marriage as a ground for divorce should be applicable to all, irrespective of religion and caste.

> **Judgment and Reasoning:**

The Supreme Court analyzed pertinent laws, including Section 13-B of the Hindu Marriage Act and Article 142(1) of the Constitution. It ruled in favor of Shilpa Sailesh, recognizing irretrievable breakdown as a valid ground for divorce and invoking Article 142(1) to dissolve the marriage. The Court emphasized equitable justice, welfare of parties, and the discretionary nature of its powers under Article 142(1). The judgment marks a significant departure from fault-based approaches to divorce, emphasizing the importance of individual well-being and fairness

➢ **Importance and Impact:**

The judgment signifies a transformative shift in family law, acknowledging evolving societal norms and prioritizing individual welfare. It emphasizes the judiciary's role in promoting equitable outcomes in marital disputes and adapting to contemporary needs. However, concerns regarding potential misuse of discretionary powers, erosion of legislative intent, and lack of clear criteria necessitate legislative clarity and a broader legal discourse on family law.

➢ **Practical Implications:**

For advocates and judges, the judgment underscores the need for a nuanced understanding of marital complexities and the exercise of judicial discretion. It calls for comprehensive criteria for the application of Article 142(1) powers and emphasizes the importance of balancing legal formalism with effective justice. Advocates should be aware of the potential impact on future cases and advocate for legislative reforms to address concerns raised by the judgment.

➢ Conclusion:

The case of Shilpa Sailesh vs Varun Sreenivasan represents a watershed moment in Indian family law, highlighting the judiciary's evolving approach to marital disputes. While the judgment prioritizes individual welfare and equitable justice, criticisms regarding potential misuse of discretionary powers and erosion of legislative intent warrant further legislative clarity and broader legal discourse. Ultimately, the judgment underscores the need for a balanced and informed approach to family law that considers evolving societal dynamics and promotes fairness and justice for all parties involved.

Scan Me to Download

Case-6

PAPER VS. POSSESSION: WHY REVENUE RECORDS ALONE CAN'T PROVE LAND OWNERSHIP

❖ P. KISHORE KUMAR ... VS. VITTAL K. PATKAR

> ➢ **Background of the Case:**

This civil appeal arises from a dispute over land in Karnataka, India. The plaintiff claims ownership based on a family settlement deed from 1953, while the defendant asserts ownership through subsequent transactions. The case revolves around the interpretation of the Mysore (Personal & Miscellaneous) Inam Abolition Act, 1954, and a Commissioner's order regarding occupancy rights.

> ➢ **Facts:**

1. The land in question, part of Sy. No. 3 in Navarathna Agrahara, was owned by the plaintiff's predecessor-in-interest.

2. The plaintiff's vendor, Smt. Akula Yogamba, sold a portion of the land to the plaintiff.

3. The Inam Abolition Act, 1954, vested land rights in the state, but allowed occupants to apply for occupancy rights.

4. The Commissioner's order from 1958 denied occupancy rights to the plaintiff's vendor.

5. Amendments in 1979 transferred the jurisdiction to grant occupancy rights to the Land Tribunal.

6. The plaintiff filed a suit for declaration of title and injunction against the defendant, claiming ownership based on the Commissioner's order and revenue records.

7. The Trial Court ruled in favor of the plaintiff, but the first appellate court overturned the decision.

8. The High Court, in a second appeal, upheld the Trial Court's decision, leading to this civil appeal.

➢ Legal Issues Involved:

1. Interpretation of the Commissioner's order regarding occupancy rights.

2. Validity of the plaintiff's claim based on revenue records.

3. Burden of proof in suits for declaration of title.

4. Application of the principle of nemo dat quod non habet (no one can transfer a better title than they possess).

➢ Court's Decision and Reasoning:

1. The Supreme Court analyzed the relevant provisions of the Inam Abolition Act and held that only tenants or Inamdars could apply for occupancy rights.

2. The Commissioner's order clearly denied occupancy rights to the plaintiff's vendor.

3. Revenue records alone cannot establish title; they only serve fiscal purposes.

4. The plaintiff's sale deed lacked evidence of a grant from the government and concealed the vendor's failed application for occupancy rights.

5. The defendant's sale deed, supported by the Commissioner's order, carried more weight.

6. The plaintiff failed to meet the burden of proof to establish title.

➢ Importance and Impact of the Judgment:

1. Clarifies the importance of documentary evidence in establishing property rights.

2. Emphasizes the principle of burden of proof in property disputes.

3. Highlights the significance of interpreting legal documents accurately.

4. Sets a precedent for future cases involving interpretation of land laws and revenue records.

➤ **Practical Implications:**

1. Advocates and judges must carefully analyze documentary evidence in property disputes.

2. Parties must ensure full disclosure of relevant documents to avoid adverse implications on their case.

3. Encourages litigants to diligently investigate and prove their title in property disputes.

➤ **Conclusion:**

The Supreme Court allowed the civil appeal, setting aside the High Court's decision and dismissing the plaintiff's suit. The judgment emphasizes the importance of accurate interpretation of legal documents and the burden of proof in property disputes. It sets a precedent for future cases involving land laws and revenue records.

Scan Me to Download

Case-7

ARREST NOT A ROUTINE: SUPREME COURT PUTS CHECKS ON DOWRY CASES
ARNESH KUMAR VS STATE OF BIHAR & ANR

➢ Background and Facts

The petitioner, a husband, is facing charges under Section 498-A of the IPC (cruelty by husband or relative of husband) and Section 4 of the Dowry Prohibition Act (demanding dowry). His wife accuses him and his relatives of demanding dowry and harassing her for not fulfilling those demands. The petitioner denies these allegations and his attempts to secure anticipatory bail were previously rejected by lower courts.

➢ Issues

1. Whether the husband should be granted anticipatory bail.

2. Whether Section 498-A of the IPC is misused by disgruntled wives.

3. How to strike a balance between protecting women from cruelty and preventing misuse of the law.

4. When can police arrest someone without a warrant?

➢ Legal Issues Involved

1. Misuse of Section 498-A of the IPC for harassing husbands and relatives.

2. Power of arrest under Section 41 of the CrPC (Code of Criminal Procedure).

3. When arrest is necessary and when a notice of appearance can suffice (Section 41A CrPC).

4. Magistrate's role in scrutinizing arrests and authorizing detention.

➢ Court's Decision and Reasoning

1. The Court granted anticipatory bail to the husband.

2. The Court highlighted the misuse of Section 498-A to harass husbands and relatives with false dowry demands.

3. The Court emphasized that arrest should not be routine and Magistrates should scrutinize the reasons for arrest.

➢ Important Points Raised in the Judgement

1. The high rate of arrest and low conviction rate under Section 498-A suggests misuse.

2. Arrests should be based on necessity and not just because an offense is cognizable and non-bailable.

3. Police officers must record reasons for arrest and Magistrates must review them for validity.

4. Section 41A of CrPC allows notice of appearance instead of arrest in many cases.

➢ Practical Implications on Advocates and Judges

1. Advocates should be aware of guidelines for arrest and detention to represent clients effectively.
2. Judges should scrutinize arrest reasons and ensure Magistrates comply with directions.

➢ Supreme Court Directions on Arrest

1. Police should not automatically arrest in dowry harassment cases.

2. Police should use checklists to ensure arrests comply with Section 41 CrPC.

3. Magistrates must review police reports and record reasons for authorizing detention.

4. Decisions not to arrest and reasons for delay in notice of appearance must be documented.

5. Non-compliance with these directions may result in departmental action or contempt charges.

➢ Conclusion

This judgement aims to prevent misuse of dowry harassment laws and ensure arrests are necessary and legal. It provides directions for police and Magistrates to improve the process and protect individual liberty. These directions apply to all cases with a maximum punishment of less than or equal to seven years.

Scan Me to Download

Case-8

TRIAL BY FIRE: DOWRY DEATH AND DOUBT IN THE COURTROOM

Phulel Singh v. State of Haryana

➢ Case Background:

This case revolves around an appeal challenging the judgment passed by the Division Bench of the High Court for the States of Punjab and Haryana. The trial court convicted the appellant under Section 304-B of the Indian Penal Code (IPC) for the dowry death of his wife, while his father was acquitted. The High Court partially allowed the appeal, acquitting the father-in-law but upholding the appellant's conviction. The deceased had allegedly been harassed for dowry, leading to her death by burning. The prosecution primarily relied on the dying declaration of the deceased.

➢ Facts:

The appellant's marriage to the deceased was marred by alleged dowry harassment. The deceased's family had provided cash, a scooter, and gold ornaments as dowry. She had informed her family about the harassment and refused to stay with the appellant. She was eventually brought back but continued to face mistreatment. On Diwali of 1991, she was found burnt, allegedly by the appellant. She made a dying declaration accusing him, which was recorded three days later.

➤ Issues:

1. Reliability of the dying declaration.

2. Existence of harassment for dowry.

3. Legality of the conviction under Section 304-B of IPC.

➤ Important Points Considered in the Judgment:

1. Evaluation of the dying declaration's credibility.

2. Doubt regarding the voluntariness of the declaration due to potential external influence.

3. Discrepancies in the timeline of events surrounding the recording of the declaration.

4. Lack of substantial evidence proving dowry harassment beyond reasonable doubt.

➤ Legal Issues Involved:

1. Admissibility and reliability of dying declarations.

2. Burden of proof in cases of dowry harassment and dowry death under IPC.

3. Standard of proof required for conviction under Section 304-B of IPC.

> ### ➢ Court's Decision and Reasoning:

The court found the dying declaration to be unreliable due to doubts regarding its voluntariness and discrepancies in the timeline of events. It also noted insufficient evidence to prove dowry harassment beyond reasonable doubt. Consequently, the conviction under Section 304-B of IPC was overturned, and the appellant was acquitted of all charges.

> ### ➢ Importance and Impact of the Judgment:

The judgment emphasizes the importance of scrutinizing dying declarations for reliability. It sets a precedent for cases involving dowry deaths, highlighting the need for substantial evidence to establish guilt beyond reasonable doubt. This decision safeguards against wrongful convictions based solely on testimonies that lack credibility or are potentially influenced.

> ### ➢ Relevant Precedents and Citations Used:

The judgment refers to the case of Makhan Singh v. State of Haryana (2022 SCC OnLine SC 1019) to illustrate principles regarding the reliability of dying declarations and the burden of proof in criminal cases.

➢ **Practical Implications on Advocates and Judges:**

Advocates must carefully scrutinize evidence, especially dying declarations, for reliability and voluntariness. Judges need to ensure that convictions are based on substantial evidence that meets the legal standards of proof. This case underscores the importance of upholding procedural fairness and adhering to legal principles in criminal proceedings.

➢ **Conclusion:**

The court's decision to acquit the appellant highlights the significance of upholding legal standards of evidence in criminal cases. It underscores the need for thorough evaluation of testimonies and evidence to ensure justice is served. This judgment serves as a precedent for future cases involving similar circumstances, guiding legal practitioners in their approach to such matters.

Scan Me to Download

Case-9

PRESUMPTION REJECTED: LANDMARK JUDGMENT IN DOWRY DEATH APPEAL

Charan Singh @ Charanjit Singh V/S The State of Uttarakhand

➢ Background of the Case:

The case revolves around the death of Chhilo Kaur, the wife of the appellant, Charan Singh. The appellant was convicted and sentenced under sections 304B, 498A, and 201 of the Indian Penal Code (IPC). The deceased's father filed a complaint alleging that she was murdered by her husband and in-laws due to non-fulfillment of dowry demands.

➢ Facts:

Chhilo Kaur was married to Charan Singh in 1993. About two years into the marriage, she returned to her parental home alleging harassment by her in-laws for not fulfilling dowry demands, including a motorcycle and land. On June 22, 1995, she was allegedly beaten and strangled to death by her husband, brother-in-law, and mother-in-law. The complaint filed by her father led to the arrest and subsequent conviction of the appellant.

➢ Legal Issues Involved:

The key legal issues include whether the death of Chhilo Kaur qualifies as a dowry death under Section 304B IPC, whether the appellant subjected her to cruelty under Section 498A IPC, and if there is evidence to support these allegations.

➤ Court's Decision and Reasoning:
The trial court convicted the appellant based on witness testimonies alleging dowry demands and harassment. However, the High Court reduced the sentence but upheld the conviction. The appellant appealed, arguing that the evidence did not support the charges against him.

The Supreme Court analyzed the evidence presented by both parties. It found that none of the witnesses testified to cruelty or harassment immediately preceding the death. The prosecution failed to establish the pre-requisites for invoking the presumption under Section 304B IPC or Section 113B of the Indian Evidence Act. As a result, the conviction could not be sustained, and the appellant's appeal was allowed.

➤ Importance and Impact of the Judgment:
This judgment highlights the importance of establishing evidence beyond reasonable doubt in cases involving dowry deaths and cruelty against married women. It underscores the need for careful consideration of witness testimonies and adherence to legal standards to prevent wrongful convictions.

➤ Relevant Precedents and Citations:

The judgment refers to the case of Baijnath v. State of M.P., which discusses the pre-requisites for raising presumption under Section 304B IPC. It also cites legal interpretations of Sections 304B, 498A, and 113B IPC from previous cases to establish the legal framework for evaluating dowry death cases.

> ➤ **Practical Implications on Advocates and Judges:**

This case emphasizes the importance of thorough examination of evidence and adherence to legal standards in cases involving dowry deaths. It serves as a precedent for future cases, guiding advocates and judges on the interpretation and application of relevant laws.

> ➤ **Conclusion:**

The Supreme Court's judgment in this case underscores the necessity of meeting legal standards and evidentiary requirements in cases of dowry deaths and cruelty against married women. It highlights the importance of establishing proof beyond reasonable doubt and adhering to legal principles to ensure justice is served.

Scan Me to Download

Case-10

THE ILLUSION OF CERTAINTY: A CASE OF UNRAVELING CONVICTIONS

MANOJ KUMAR SONI VS. THE STATE OF MADHYA PRADESH

➢ **Background of the Case:**

The case involves the convictions of Manoj and Kallu for their alleged involvement in a criminal conspiracy and receiving stolen property. The prosecution's case primarily relied on disclosure statements made by the accused and co-accused individuals, leading to the recovery of stolen articles. However, doubts were raised regarding the adequacy and reliability of these statements, as well as the credibility of the seizure witnesses.

➢ **Facts:**

1. The accused, along with co-accused individuals, were implicated in a case involving theft and sale of stolen articles.

2. The prosecution's case was built on disclosure statements made by the accused and co-accused, leading to the recovery of stolen property.

3. Seizure witnesses who were present during the recovery of stolen articles turned hostile, casting doubt on the credibility of the seizures.

4. The Trial Court convicted Manoj and Kallu based on these disclosure statements and the presumption under Section 114(a) of the Evidence Act regarding possession of stolen property.

> Issues:

1. Whether disclosure statements made by the accused and co-accused were sufficient evidence to secure convictions.

2. The credibility and reliability of seizure witnesses and their impact on the prosecution's case.

3. Whether the Trial Court erred in framing questions during examination under Section 313, Cr.PC.

4. The validity of convictions under Section 411 (receiving stolen property) and Section 120-B (criminal conspiracy) of the IPC.

> Important Points Considered in the Judgment:

1. The evidentiary value of disclosure statements under Section 27 of the Evidence Act.

2. The significance of corroborating evidence and the credibility of seizure witnesses.

3. Proper procedure during examination under Section 313, Cr.PC.

4. Interpretation of Section 411 and Section 120-B of the IPC.

5. Adherence to established legal principles and precedents in criminal cases.

➤ Court's Decision and Reasoning:

The court acquitted Manoj and Kallu, citing insufficient evidence to justify their convictions. It emphasized the flaws in the prosecution's case, including overreliance on disclosure statements and the lack of credible corroborating evidence. The court also highlighted procedural errors during examination under Section 313, Cr.PC, and questioned the validity of convictions under Section 411 and Section 120-B of the IPC. Ultimately, the court concluded that the convictions could not be sustained based on illusionary knowledge and lack of credible evidence.

➤ Importance and Impact of the Judgment:

The judgment underscores the importance of adhering to legal principles and ensuring the reliability of evidence in criminal cases. It highlights the need for corroborating evidence to support prosecution's claims and emphasizes the limitations of relying solely on disclosure statements. The decision sets a precedent for future cases involving similar issues of evidentiary value and procedural fairness.

➤ Relevant Precedents and Citations Used:

1. Pulukuri Kotayya and others vs. King-Emperor (Privy Council)

2. Emperor vs. Lalit Mohan Chuckerburty

3. Haricharan Kurmi vs. State of Bihar

4. Shiv Kumar vs. State of Madhya Pradesh

5. Sanjeet Kumar Singh vs. State of Chhattisgarh

6. A Devendran vs. State of Tamil Nadu

7. The King vs. Plummer

8. I.G. Singleton v. King-Emperor

➤ Practical Implications on Advocates and Judges:

The judgment serves as a reminder for advocates to ensure the credibility and reliability of evidence presented in court. It also highlights the importance of thorough investigation and adherence to procedural fairness. For judges, the case underscores the need to critically evaluate the evidence and apply established legal principles in reaching decisions.

➢ **Conclusion of the Case:**

Manoj and Kallu were acquitted, and their convictions were set aside due to the lack of sufficient evidence and procedural errors. The judgment emphasizes the importance of upholding the principles of justice and ensuring the integrity of the legal process in criminal cases.

Scan Me to Download

Case-11

NECESSITY VS. CONVENIENCE: COURT DENIES EASEMENT CLAIM IN LAND DISPUTE

MANISHA MAHENDRA GALA & ORS V/S SHALINI BHAGWAN AVATRAMANI & ORS.

➢ Background Of The Case

This dispute involves two appeals concerning easement rights over a 20-foot wide road situated on land identified by Survey No. 57 Hissa No. 13A/1, currently owned by the respondents (referred to as 'Ramani's' hereinafter).

The dispute arose when Joki Woler Ruzer (original plaintiff) and his successors, the Gala's, who own the land designated Survey No. 48 Hissa No. 15, claimed easement rights over the aforementioned road.

➢ Facts of the Case

1. Joki Woler Ruzer filed Suit No. 14 of 1994, seeking a declaration of his easement rights and a permanent injunction to protect those rights.

2. The trial court ruled in favor of the Gala's in 2003.

3. This decision was overturned on appeal by the Ad-hoc District Judge-2 in 2009.

4. The High Court upheld the appellate court's decision in 2009.

5. The Gala's filed these appeals challenging both the dismissal of their suit and the decree in favor of the Ramani's in Suit No. 7 of 1996.

6. The Ramani's had filed Suit No. 7 of 1996 to claim that the Gala's have no right of way through the disputed land.

7. The trial court ruled in favor of the Gala's in 2003, but this decision was reversed on appeal in 2009.

➤ **Issues Involved**

1. Whether the Gala's possess easement rights over the road on the Ramani's property.

2. Whether the Sale Deed dated 17.09.1994 granted the Gala's easement rights.

➤ **Important Points Considered in the Judgement**

1. The definition of an easement under the Indian Easements Act, 1882.

2. Requirements for acquiring an easement by prescription under Section 15 of the Act.

3. The ability of a Power of Attorney holder to act as a witness.

4. Easements by necessity as defined by Section 13 of the Act.

5. Admissibility of evidence (photocopy vs. original Sale Deed).

> **Court's Decision and Reasoning**

The Court ruled in favor of the Ramani's, reasoning that the Gala's failed to establish their claim to an easement. Here's a breakdown of the Court's reasoning:

1. **Easement by Prescription:** The Gala's pleadings did not specifically claim they or their predecessors had used the road for over 20 years, a requirement under Section 15 of the Act for acquiring an easement by prescription.

2. **Power of Attorney Holder's Testimony:** The Gala's Power of Attorney holder lacked the necessary knowledge to establish a pre-existing right, as they only entered the scene after the suit was filed.

3. **Easement by Necessity:** The Gala's had an alternative way to access their land, negating the claim of necessity.

4. **Sale Deed:** The Sale Deed did not grant the Gala's any easement rights they could not have already possessed. The predecessor-in-interest did not establish such rights before the sale.

> ➢ **Importance and Impact of the Judgement**

This judgement clarifies the legal requirements for acquiring easement rights, specifically by prescription and necessity. It also emphasizes the limitations of a Power of Attorney holder's role in litigation.
Relevant Precedents and Citations Used

1. Ram Sarup Gupta (Dead) By Lrs. vs. Bishun Narain Inter College & Ors (1987) 2 SCC 555

2. Janki Vashdeo Bhojwani vs. IndusInd Bank Ltd. (2005) 2 SCC 217

3. A.C Narayan vs. State of Maharashtra (2014) 11 SCC 790

4. Dr. S. Kumar & Ors. vs. S. Ramalingam (2020) 16 SCC 553

> ➢ **Practical Implications on Advocates and Judges**

1. Advocates must ensure pleadings precisely comply with statutory requirements for acquiring easements.

2. Courts should scrutinize the knowledge and qualifications of witnesses, particularly Power of Attorney holders.

➢ **Conclusion**

The Court dismissed the appeals, upholding the rights of the Ramani's as owners of the land and rejecting the Gala's claims to easement rights. This case clarifies the legal requirements for acquiring easements and the limitations of Power of Attorney holders in litigation.

Scan Me to Download

Case-12

PRESUMPTION, PROOF, AND THE PEN: A CASE OF REBUTTABLE DOUBT
K. Subramani ... V/S K. Damodara Naidu

> ➤ **Background of the Case:**

The complainant and the accused were working as lecturers in a Government college at Bangalore. The complainant alleged that the accused borrowed a loan of Rs. 14 lakhs from him in cash on 1.12.1997 to start granite business. The accused issued a post-dated cheque dated 30.11.2000 for Rs. 29,12,000/- which included principal and interest. The cheque was dishonored with an endorsement 'fund insufficient' and the complainant lodged a complaint under Section 138 of the Negotiable Instrument Act against the accused.

The trial court held that the complainant had no source of income to lend a sum of Rs. 14 lakhs to the accused and he failed to prove that there is a legally recoverable debt payable by the accused to him. The trial court acquitted the accused.

> **Issues:**

1. Whether an action under Section 138 of the N.I. Act for dishonor of cheque requires the complainant to establish his financial capacity to lend money?
2. Will the presumption under Section 139 of the N.I. Act accrue to the benefit of the complainant unless the accused rebuts that presumption?

The High Court set aside the judgment of acquittal passed by the trial court and remanded the case to the trial court for retrial.

The Supreme Court allowed the appeal and restored the judgment of acquittal passed by the trial court.

> **Important Points Considered in the Judgement:**

1. Presumption under Section 139 of the N.I. Act: The presumption under Section 139 of the N.I. Act is a rebuttable presumption. The accused can rebut the presumption by proving that there is no legally recoverable debt.

2. Source of income of the complainant: The complainant claimed that the source of the loan was his savings from salary and an amount of Rs. 5 lakhs derived by him from

sale of site No. 45 belonging to him. However, the complainant did not produce any documents to substantiate his claim.

3. Government Servants' Conduct Rules: The complainant and the accused were governed by the Government Servants' Conduct Rules which prescribes the mode of lending and borrowing. There is nothing on record to show that the prescribed mode was followed.

> **Legal Issues Involved:**

1. Whether an action under Section 138 of the N.I. Act for dishonor of cheque requires the complainant to establish his financial capacity to lend money?

2. Will the presumption under Section 139 of the N.I. Act accrue to the benefit of the complainant unless the accused rebuts that presumption?

> **Court's Decision and Reasoning:**

The presumption under Section 139 of the N.I. Act is a rebuttable presumption. The accused can rebut the presumption by proving that there is no legally recoverable debt. The court also held that the complainant failed to prove that he had the financial capacity to lend Rs. 14 lakhs to the accused.

The reasoning of the court is as follows: The trial court held that the complainant had no source of income to lend a sum of Rs. 14 lakhs to the accused and he failed to prove that there is a legally recoverable debt payable by the accused to him. The Supreme Court agreed with the reasoning of the trial court.

➢ Importance and Impact of the Judgement:

It clarifies that the presumption under Section 139 of the N.I. Act is rebuttable. The accused can contest the existence of a legally enforceable debt.

➢ Practical Implications on Advocates and Judges:

1. Advocates appearing for the complainant in cases under Section 138 of the N.I. Act must be prepared to prove that the complainant has the financial capacity to lend the amount of the cheque.

Judges presiding over cases under Section 138 of the N.I. Act should carefully consider the evidence relating to the complainant's financial capacity to lend the amount of the cheque

➢ **Conclusion**

The conclusion of this case is that the Supreme Court restored the judgment of acquittal passed by the trial court

- ✓ Here's a breakdown of how the case reached this conclusion

The trial court initially aquitted the accused because the complainant (the other lecturer) couldn't prove he had the financial means to lend such a large sum (Rs. 14 lakhs).

The High Court disagreed and remanded the case for retrial, believing the presumption of debt under the Negotiable Instruments Act applied

The Supreme Court ultimately sided with the trial court.

Therefore, the accused was acquitted as the prosecution couldn't establish a legally recoverable debt

Scan Me to Download

Case-13

TIME OF THE ESSENCE: COURT DENIES LAND TRANSFER DUE TO LATE PAYMENT

SMT. KATTA SUJATHA REDDY & ANR. V/S SIDDAMSETTY INFRA PROJECTS PVT. LTD.& ORS

➢ A Detailed Case Background and Facts

This case involves a dispute over a land sale agreement between a purchaser (Sunil Siddam Setty) and vendors (Katta Sujatha Reddy and others). In 1997, the parties entered into agreements for the sale of a property, with a clause mandating completion within three months and full payment by the purchaser. The purchaser made a partial payment initially, but there was a subsequent delay in paying the remaining balance.

❖ The Agreement and Timeline:

- In March 1997, the purchaser and vendors signed agreements for the sale of a specific property.

- A crucial clause in the agreements stipulated that the entire transaction, including full payment from the purchaser, had to be completed within three months

Payment Issues and Delays:

- The purchaser made an initial partial payment upon signing the agreement.
- However, they failed to pay the remaining balance within the designated three-month timeframe.

Escalation to Legal Action:

- Due to the purchaser's delay in completing the payment, the vendors did not execute the sale deed, transferring ownership of the land.

- Years later, the purchaser filed a lawsuit seeking specific performance of the contract. Specific performance is a legal remedy that compels a party to fulfill their contractual obligations.

New Legislation and its Impact:

- In 2018, an amendment was introduced to the Specific Relief Act, potentially affecting the approach to specific performance in some cases.

> **Issues Raised**

1.Limitation: Whether the purchaser's lawsuit for specific performance, filed several years after the stipulated completion date, was barred by the limitation period.

2.Retrospective Application of Amendment: Whether a 2018 amendment to the Specific Relief Act, making specific performance mandatory in some cases, applied to this pre-2018 agreement.

3.Purchaser's Entitlement to Relief: Whether the purchaser was entitled to specific performance of the contract, considering the delay in payment.

4.Benefit of Partial Payment: Whether the purchaser could claim a portion of the land proportionate to the partial payment made.

> ➢ **Legal Issues Involved**
> - ***Contract Law:*** Interpretation of the agreement's terms, specifically the "time of the essence" clause and the purchaser's obligations.
>
> - ***Specific Relief Act:*** Applicability of Section 16(c) regarding the purchaser's "readiness and willingness" to perform the contract.
>
> - ***Limitation Act:*** Application of the limitation period for filing suits for specific performance.
>
> - ***Statutory Interpretation:*** Whether the 2018 amendment to the Specific Relief Act applied retrospectively.
>
> ➢ **Court's Decision and Reasoning**

The court ruled in favor of the vendors on all points. Here's the reasoning behind each issue:

- *Limitation:* The court held the suit time-barred as the purchaser did not file it within the three-year limitation period prescribed by the Limitation Act, and the delay in payment constituted a breach of the contract.

- *Retrospective Application:* The 2018 amendment modifying the approach to specific performance was deemed not applicable to pre-2018 agreements. The court differentiated between procedural and substantive changes, and since the amendment created new rights and obligations, it wasn't applied retrospectively.

- *Purchaser's Entitlement:* The court denied specific performance due to the purchaser's failure to adhere to the time clause and lack of demonstrable "readiness and willingness" to perform. The purchaser's inaction within the stipulated timeframe constituted a breach.

- *Benefit of Partial Payment*: Section 12 of the Specific Relief Act, which allows for specific performance of a part of a contract under certain conditions, was deemed inapplicable. The court reasoned that the purchaser's own breach caused the issue, and their delay further disqualified them from relief under this section.

➢ **Important Points Considered:**

- The court emphasized the importance of adhering to contractual timelines, especially when a clause explicitly makes time of the essence.

- The burden of proving "readiness and willingness" to perform lies with the purchaser.

- The court distinguished between procedural and substantive amendments to legislation when considering retrospective application.

-

➤ Precedents and Citations Used

- **Chand Rani [(1993) 1 SCC 519]**: Cited to support the principle of "time of the essence" in contracts relating to immovable property.

- **Saradamani Kandappan v. S. Rajalakshmi and other [(2011) 12 SCC 18]**: Referred to for the court's discretion in granting specific performance and the importance of considering adherence to timelines.

- **Jaswinder Kaur v. Gurmeet Singh [(2017) 12 SCC 810]**: Explained the scope of Section 12 of the Specific Relief Act regarding specific performance of parts of a contract.

➤ Practical Implications for Advocates and Judges
- **Contract Drafting:** Advocates should ensure clear and unambiguous language when drafting clauses regarding timelines and consequences of non-performance in contracts.

- **Evidence Gathering:** For specific performance claims, advocates for the purchaser must establish clear evidence of "readiness and willingness" to perform the contract.

- **Retrospective Application:** Judges should carefully analyze the nature of amendments to determine whether they are procedural or substantive when considering their retrospective application.

➤ **Importance and Impact of the Judgment**

This case reaffirms the significance of adhering to contractual timelines and the court's discretion in granting specific performance. It also clarifies the limited applicability of Section 12 of the Specific Relief Act in cases where the purchaser's breach caused the impossibility of complete performance.

➤ **Conclusion**

The court ultimately protected the vendors' rights by denying specific performance due to the purchaser's breach of contract. This judgment serves as a reminder for parties involved in agreements to strictly adhere to their terms and conditions, particularly when timelines are explicitly designated as crucial.

Scan Me to Download

Case-14

DEFINING "PIOUS PURPOSE": COURT CLARIFIES LIMITS ON GIFTING ANCESTRAL PROPERTY

❖ K.C. LAXMANA VERSUS K.C. CHANDRAPPA GOWDA & ANR

➢ **Background of the Case**

This case involves a dispute over a joint family property governed by Mitakshara Law. The plaintiff (KC Chandrappa Gowda) sued his father (KC Chinne Gowda) and another defendant (KC Laxmana) to partition the property and declare a gift deed executed by his father in favor of Laxmana as void.

The story revolves around a Hindu Undivided Family (HUF) consisting of three coparceners: KC Chandrappa Gowda (plaintiff), his father KC Chinne Gowda (1st defendant), and another son, Subraya Gowda. The HUF owned a piece of property, considered ancestral under Mitakshara Law. This law governs the inheritance and ownership of property in certain Hindu communities.

A conflict arose when the father, KC Chinne Gowda, executed a gift deed in favor of KC Laxmana (2nd defendant). This essentially transferred a portion of the joint family property to Laxmana. Here's where the issues begin:

- *Lack of Consent:* The plaintiff, Chandrappa Gowda, vehemently opposed this move. He claimed he never consented to the gift, implying a violation of his rights as a coparcener who holds equal ownership rights in the property.

- *"Pious Purpose" Defense:* The 2nd defendant, Laxmana, defended the gift by claiming it served a "pious purpose." He argued that the 1st defendant raised him, even though Laxmana wasn't a blood relative. However, the exact nature of this "pious purpose" remained unclear.

➢ **Facts of the Case**
- The property belonged to a joint family consisting of the plaintiff, his father, and another son (Subraya Gowda).

- The father (1st defendant) gifted the property to Laxmana (2nd defendant) through a deed.

- The plaintiff claimed he did not consent to the gift and challenged it as being beyond his father's authority.

- The 2nd defendant argued the property was already partitioned, and the gift was for a "pious purpose" (out of love and affection for raising him).

➢ **Legal Questions and the Applicable Framework:**

The case raised several legal questions that needed to be addressed by the court:

- *Time Limit for Challenge:* The Limitation Act in India sets time limits for filing various lawsuits. The court had to determine the relevant article applicable to this case. Two possibilities arose:

    - Article 58: This is a general provision with a 3-year limit for seeking a declaration (a legal statement confirming rights).
    - Article 109: This specific article applies to Mitakshara Law and allows a son to challenge his father's alienation (transfer) of ancestral property within 12 years of the recipient taking possession.

- *Karta's Authority:* The court needed to clarify the extent of the Karta's (father's) power to dispose of joint family property. This power is generally limited to specific situations:

Legal necessity (e.g., paying off a debt)

Benefit of the estate (e.g., repairs)

With the consent of all coparceners

- *"Pious Purpose" Defined:* The meaning of "pious purpose" in the context of gifting ancestral property was crucial. Does it extend beyond religious or charitable purposes to encompass acts of "love and affection" for someone outside the family?

➢ **Issues Involved**

- Whether the suit filed by the plaintiff was barred by limitation.

- Whether the transfer of property by the father to the 2nd defendant was for a valid purpose.

> **Important Points Considered in the Judgement**

- The Limitation Act and the relevant articles for challenging property alienation.

- The concept of coparcenary in a Mitakshara Law governed joint family.

- The authority of the Karta (manager) to dispose of joint family property.

- The meaning of "pious purpose" in the context of gifting ancestral property.

> **Legal Issues Involved**

Applicability of Limitation Act - Article 58 (general declaration) vs. Article 109 (challenge to father's alienation by son).

Authority of the Karta to gift joint family property - necessity for consent of coparceners and valid purpose.

> **Court's Decision and Reasoning**

- ✓ The court ruled the suit was not barred by limitation as Article 109 of the Limitation Act applied (12 years from alienee taking possession).

- ✓ The court held the gift deed was void as it wasn't for a legal necessity, benefit of the estate, or with the consent of all coparceners.

- ✓ "Pious purpose" for gifting ancestral property was limited to charitable or religious purposes, not "love and affection" for a non-coparcener.

The court cited previous judgements (Thimmaiah vs. Ningamma & Guramma vs. Mallappa) to support its reasoning.

> **Importance and Impact of the Judgement**

- This judgement clarifies the limitations on the Karta's power to gift joint family property.

- It emphasizes the need for coparceners' consent for such transactions.

- The judgement defines the scope of "pious purpose" for gifting ancestral property.
> **Relevant Precedents and Citations Used**

❖ Thimmaiah and Ors. Vs. Ningamma and Anr. (2000) 7 SCC 409

❖ Guramma Bhratar Chanbasappa Deshmukh and Ors. vs. Mallappa Chanbasappa and Anr. AIR 1964 SC 510

❖ Ammathayi @ Perumalakkal and Anr. Vs. Kumaresan @ Balakrishnan and Ors. AIR 1967 SC 569

> **Practical Implications on Advocates and Judges**

- Advocates must carefully consider the specific articles under the Limitation Act for property disputes.

- Judges need to assess the purpose and consent involved in property alienation by the Karta.

> **Conclusion**

This case reinforces the restrictions on a Karta's power to dispose of joint family property. It highlights the importance of coparceners' consent and the limited scope of "pious purpose" for gifting ancestral property. The judgement provides valuable guidance for advocates and judges dealing with similar cases.

Scan Me to Download

Case-15

CLEARING THE CONFUSION: SUPREME COURT STREAMLINES MAINTENANCE PROCESS

❖ RAJNESH ...V/S NEHA & ANR.

➢ Background of the Case

The wife filed an application under Section 125 of the Cr.P.C. seeking interim maintenance for herself and her minor son after leaving the matrimonial home. The Family Court awarded interim maintenance, which was challenged by the husband before the High Court and then the Supreme Court.

➢ Facts

o The wife left the matrimonial home in 2013 shortly after the birth of their son.

o In 2013, the wife filed an application under Section 125 of the Cr.P.C. for interim maintenance.

- The Family Court awarded interim maintenance of Rs. 15,000 per month to the wife and Rs. 5,000 per month for the son (increasing to Rs. 10,000 per month later).

- The husband challenged the order in the High Court and then the Supreme Court.

> **Issues**

- Whether the wife is entitled to interim maintenance.

- Whether the amount of maintenance awarded by the Family Court is appropriate.

> **Important Points Raised in the Judgement**

- The Supreme Court upheld the Family Court's order awarding interim maintenance.

- The Court emphasized the need for uniformity and consistency in deciding maintenance applications.

- The Court issued guidelines on various aspects of maintenance payments in matrimonial matters.

➢ **Legal Issues Involved**

- Interpretation of Section 125 of the Cr.P.C.
- Principles for determining the quantum of maintenance.
- Enforcement of maintenance orders.

➢ **Court's Decision and Reasoning**

- The Supreme Court affirmed the Family Court's order on interim maintenance.
- The Court held that maintenance should be awarded from the date of filing the application.
- The Court issued guidelines on disclosure of assets, criteria for determining maintenance amount, and enforcement of orders.

❖ *The Supreme Court, after considering various aspects of the case, has issued the following directions under Article 142 of the Constitution of India to ensure fairness and uniformity in matrimonial case*

<u>1. Issue of Overlapping Jurisdiction:</u>

  o To avoid conflicting orders in different proceedings, courts must:

- Adjust or set-off maintenance amounts awarded in previous proceedings when determining further awards.

- Mandate applicants to disclose previous proceedings and orders in subsequent cases.

- Modify or vary orders from previous proceedings within the same proceeding.

2. Payment of Interim Maintenance:

- Both parties must file an Affidavit of Disclosure of Assets and Liabilities in all maintenance proceedings, including pending cases in Family Courts, District Courts, or Magistrates Courts.

3. Criteria for Determining Maintenance Amount:

- Courts shall consider factors listed in the judgment for determining maintenance.
- Courts have discretion to consider additional factors relevant to the case.

4. Date from Which Maintenance is Awarded:

Maintenance will be awarded from the date of filing the application for maintenance.

5. Enforcement of Maintenance Orders:

- Maintenance orders may be enforced under relevant laws such as Section 28A of the Hindu Marriage Act, 1956; Section 20(6) of the Domestic Violence Act; and Section 128 of the Criminal Procedure Code.

- Maintenance orders may be enforced as money decrees of civil courts according to the Civil Procedure Code, particularly Sections 51, 55, 58, and 60 in conjunction with Order XXI.

❖ *These directions aim to streamline procedures, promote transparency, and ensure effective enforcement of maintenance orders in matrimonial cases throughout the country.Importance and Impact of the Judgement*

- This judgement provides clear guidelines for courts to follow in maintenance cases.

- It promotes uniformity and consistency in awarding maintenance.

- It clarifies the date from which maintenance is payable.

- It strengthens the enforcement mechanisms for maintenance orders.

➢ Practical Implications on Advocates and Judges

- Advocates and judges will need to be familiar with the new guidelines issued by the Supreme Court.

- The guidelines require mandatory disclosure of assets and liabilities by both parties.

- Courts will need to consider past maintenance awards while determining subsequent awards.

➢ Conclusion

This judgement is a landmark decision that provides much-needed clarity and guidance on maintenance cases in India. The guidelines issued by the Supreme Court will promote fairness, efficiency, and uniformity in the judicial process.

Scan Me to Download

Case-16

FORGET THE PAST, FOCUS ON FACTS: QUASHING AN FIR BASED ON MERIT

MOHAMMAD WAJID & ANR. ... VERSUS STATE OF U.P. & ORS

➢ BACKGROUND OF THE CASE

The case revolves around an appeal by the original accused, numbered 1 and 2 respectively, against the First Information Report (FIR) filed under Crime Registration No. 224 of 2022 on September 19, 2022, with the Mirzapur Police Station in District Saharanpur, State of Uttar Pradesh. The FIR alleges offenses punishable under Sections 395 (robbery), 504 (intentional insult with intent to provoke breach of the peace), 506 (criminal intimidation), and 323 (voluntarily causing hurt) of the Indian Penal Code (IPC). The appeal challenges the order of the High Court of Judicature at Allahabad, dated October 17, 2022, in the Criminal Miscellaneous Writ Petition No. 15174 of 2022, which declined to quash the aforementioned FIR.

➢ FACTS
- The FIR alleged that the accused forcefully demanded land belonging to the complainant and his brother.
- The FIR was lodged in September 2022, but the alleged incident occurred sometime in 2021.
- The FIR did not mention the specific date or time of the incident.

➢ ISSUES
- Whether the FIR should be quashed due to delay in filing and vague allegations.
- Whether the appellants' criminal history can be a reason to reject the quashing of the FIR.

➢ IMPORTANT POINTS CONSIDERED IN THE JUDGEMENT
- The court's duty to scrutinize FIRs alleging frivolous or vexatious complaints.
- Delay in filing the FIR and its impact on the accused's ability to defend themselves.
- The limited role of criminal antecedents in quashing FIRs.
- Balancing the need for law enforcement with protection from harassment.

> **LEGAL ISSUES INVOLVED**

- Power of the court under Section 482 of the CrPC to quash FIRs.
- When can an FIR be considered an abuse of process.

> **COURT'S DECISION AND REASONING**

The court in this case ruled in favor of the appellants, quashing the FIR filed against them. Here's a breakdown of the court's decision and the reasoning behind it:

Decision:

The court **allowed the appeal** filed by Mohammad Wajid and the other appellant. This means the FIR lodged by Ram Kumar accusing them of various offenses was quashed (declared invalid).

Reasoning:

The court's reasoning focused on protecting the accused from potential harassment due to a weak FIR and ensuring a fair trial process. Here are the key points considered:

- **Duty to Scrutinize FIRs:** The court acknowledged its responsibility to examine FIRs with care, especially when there's a possibility of frivolous or vexatious complaints lodged with malicious intent.

- **Impact of Delay:** The significant delay in filing the FIR (September 2022 for an alleged incident in 2021) was a major factor. The court highlighted the difficulty the accused faced in defending themselves

-
- without a specific timeframe for the alleged offenses. Their alibi or whereabouts for the unspecified period couldn't be established.

- **Importance of Specificity:** The court emphasized the importance of a clear and specific FIR. The lack of a specific date and time for the alleged incident rendered the FIR vague and inadequate. This vagueness made it challenging to determine the exact nature of the offenses and when they supposedly happened.

- **Criminal History Not Sole Factor:** The court clarified that the appellants' past criminal record couldn't be the sole justification for rejecting their appeal. An FIR with weak allegations and lacking crucial details cannot be upheld simply because the accused has a history of criminal cases.

- **Balancing Rights:** The court emphasized the need to balance law enforcement's right to investigate crimes with protecting individuals from harassment through unfounded accusations. A promptly filed and specific FIR ensures a fair and balanced process.

> **IMPORTANCE AND IMPACT OF THE JUDGEMENT**

This judgement emphasizes that FIRs should be specific and filed promptly. It protects citizens from harassment due to frivolous complaints lodged with an ulterior motive.

➢ RELEVANT PRECEDENTS AND CITATIONS USED

- State of Andhra Pradesh v. Golconda Linga Swamy (2004) 6 SCC 522

- R.P. Kapur v. State of Punjab, AIR 1960 SC 866

- Bhajan Lal v. State of Haryana, (1992) 1 SCC 338

- Directorate of Revenue and another v. Mohammed Nisar Holia, (2008) 2 SCC 370

➢ PRACTICAL IMPLICATIONS ON ADVOCATES AND JUDGES

- Advocates must carefully draft FIRs to ensure they meet the legal requirements.
- Judges should scrutinize FIRs for vagueness and delay, especially when considering quashing them.

➤ CONCLUSION

This case highlights the importance of proper FIR filing procedures and protects individuals from facing trial based on weak accusations.

Scan Me to Download

Case-17

NO TURNING BACK: WHY AMENDING A SUIT CAN'T CHANGE ITS NATURE
BASAVARAJ ..VERSUS INDIRA AND OTHERS

➢ BACKGROUND OF THE CASE

The case revolves around a dispute concerning ancestral property. Respondents No. 1 and 2 (plaintiffs) filed Original Suit No. 151 of 2005 seeking partition of their grandfather's ancestral property. They later sought to amend their plaint to declare an earlier compromise decree dated October 14, 2004, as null and void. The Trial Court dismissed their application for amendment, but the High Court of Karnataka, Circuit Bench at Gulbarga, overturned this decision, allowing the amendment subject to costs. The appellants (defendants) challenged this order, leading to the current proceedings.

➢ FACTS

- *Initial Suit:* Respondents No. 1 and 2 filed a suit in 2005 for partition of ancestral property.

- *Compromise Decree:* A compromise decree was passed on October 14, 2004, in Original Suit No. 401 of 2003 by Lok Adalat, involving the same parties.

- *Amendment Application:* At the argument stage of the 2005 suit, respondents No. 1 and 2 sought to amend the plaint to challenge the 2004 compromise decree, claiming oversight and mistake for not including the declaration earlier.

- *Trial Court Decision:* The Trial Court dismissed the application for amendment.

- *High Court Decision:* The High Court reversed the Trial Court's decision, allowing the amendment.

- *Appellant's Argument:* The appellant argued that the suit's nature would change from partition to declaration, which is impermissible, and that the amendment application was time-barred and lacked due diligence.

➢ **ISSUES**

1. Whether the amendment to include the declaration that the compromise decree is null and void is permissible.

2. Whether the amendment application was filed with due diligence as required by Order VI Rule 17 CPC.

3. Whether allowing the amendment would cause prejudice to the appellants.

> ➤ **IMPORTANT POINTS CONSIDERED IN THE JUDGMENT**
1. *Change in Suit's Nature:* Allowing the amendment would change the suit's nature from partition to a declaration, which was deemed impermissible.

2. *Due Diligence:* The respondents failed to demonstrate due diligence in seeking the amendment. The oversight claimed did not meet the criteria set by the law.

3. *Prejudice to Appellants:* Allowing the amendment would prejudice the appellants as it would change the fundamental nature of the suit and negate the earlier compromise decree.

4. *Timeliness of Amendment:* The application for amendment was filed more than five years after the compromise decree, making it time-barred.

> ➤ **LEGAL ISSUES INVOLVED**
1. Permissibility of Amendments Post-Commencement of Trial:Under Order VI Rule 17 CPC, amendments post-trial commencement require demonstrating due diligence, which was not shown here.

2. Validity of Compromise Decree: The decree passed by Lok Adalat is binding unless set aside by the court that recorded it.

3. Res Judicata: The compromise decree created a res judicata, preventing the same issue from being litigated again.

> ## COURT'S DECISION AND REASONING

The Supreme Court set aside the High Court's order and dismissed the amendment application. The court held:

- Lack of Due Diligence: The respondents failed to demonstrate due diligence.

- Change in Nature of Suit: The amendment would impermissibly change the suit's nature.

- Prejudice to Appellants: Allowing the amendment would unfairly prejudice the appellants by challenging the compromise decree long after it was passed.

- Time-Barred: The amendment was time-barred as it was sought more than three years after the compromise decree.

➢ IMPORTANCE AND IMPACT OF THE JUDGMENT

- **Reaffirmation of Procedural Rules:** The judgment emphasizes the strict adherence to procedural rules under Order VI Rule 17 CPC.
- **Integrity of Compromise Decrees:** It upholds the binding nature of compromise decrees and restricts the avenues for challenging them.
- **Due Diligence Requirement:** Highlights the importance of demonstrating due diligence when seeking amendments after the trial has commenced.

➢ RELEVANT PRECEDENTS AND CITATIONS

1. Pushpa Devi Bhagat v. Rajinder Singh (2006) 5 SCC 566: Discussed the binding nature of consent decrees and the limited grounds for challenging them.

2. M. Revanna v. Anjanamma (2019) 4 SCC 332: Addressed the principles governing amendments, emphasizing the need for due diligence and the prevention of fundamental changes to the suit.

3. Revajeetu Builders v. Narayanaswamy (2009) 10 SCC 84: Listed factors to consider in amendment applications, particularly the impact on the other party and the nature of the suit.

➢ PRACTICAL IMPLICATIONS FOR ADVOCATES AND JUDGES

- ✓ Advocates: Must ensure thorough initial pleadings to avoid the need for amendments, particularly after the trial has commenced.

- ✓ Judges: Should rigorously evaluate amendment applications against the due diligence requirement and the potential impact on the nature of the suit and the other parties involved.

> **CONCLUSION**

The Supreme Court's decision underscores the importance of adhering to procedural rules in civil litigation. It reinforces the finality and binding nature of compromise decrees and the necessity of demonstrating due diligence when seeking to amend pleadings after the trial has begun. The ruling provides clarity on the application of Order VI Rule 17 CPC, serving as a significant precedent for future cases involving similar issues.

Scan Me to Download

Case-18

PROCEDURAL CLARITY: PMLA AND CRPC INTERSECT

TARSEMLAL VERSUS
DIRECTORATE OF ENFORCEMENT

> Background of the Case

This case involves the interpretation and application of various provisions under the Prevention of Money Laundering Act (PMLA), 2002, particularly in the context of criminal procedure. The primary issue revolves around whether the provisions of the Code of Criminal Procedure (CrPC), 1973, especially those concerning bail and custody, are applicable to proceedings under the PMLA.

> Facts

The case was brought before the Special Court constituted under the PMLA. The appellants, accused of committing offenses under Section 3 of the PMLA, challenged the applicability of CrPC provisions in their proceedings. They contended that once they appeared before the Special Court pursuant to a summons, they should not be deemed to be in custody, and the provisions for bail under the CrPC should apply.

➤ Issues

1. Applicability of CrPC Provisions: Whether the procedural aspects of the CrPC, such as those concerning bail and bonds, apply to PMLA proceedings.

2. Custody Definition: Whether an accused, upon appearance in response to a summons, can be deemed to be in custody under PMLA.

3. Section 88 of CrPC: Whether Section 88 of the CrPC, which deals with the power to take bonds for appearance, applies to an accused in PMLA cases.

➤ Important Points Considered in the Judgment

1. Section 46 of PMLA: This section states that the provisions of the CrPC shall apply to proceedings before a Special Court unless otherwise provided in the PMLA.

2. Prima Facie Case: The court emphasized that the Special Court must apply its mind to determine whether a prima facie case of an offense under the PMLA is made out before proceeding further.

3. Section 88 of CrPC: The Court examined whether this section, which allows courts to take bonds from individuals for their appearance, could be applied to those accused under the PMLA.

➤ Legal Issues Involved

1. Interplay between PMLA and CrPC: The primary legal issue is understanding how the procedural aspects of the CrPC integrate with the substantive provisions of the PMLA.

2. Judicial Discretion: The extent of judicial discretion in applying CrPC provisions in PMLA cases, especially concerning bail and custody.

3. Statutory Interpretation: The interpretation of the phrase "save as otherwise provided in this Act" in Section 46 of the PMLA.

➤ Court's Decision and Reasoning

1. Applicability of CrPC: The provisions of the CrPC do apply to proceedings under the PMLA, including those relating to bail and bonds.

2. Custody Definition: Merely appearing before the court in response to a summons does not amount to being in custody.

3. Section 88 of CrPC: This section applies to PMLA proceedings, and it provides discretionary power to the court to take bonds for ensuring the appearance of the accused.

The Court reasoned that Section 46 of the PMLA explicitly integrates the CrPC into its procedural framework, except where explicitly overridden by the PMLA. Hence, provisions like

Sections 88, 200 to 204 of the CrPC are applicable to PMLA cases.

➤ Importance and Impact of the Judgment

This judgment clarifies the procedural landscape for PMLA cases, ensuring that the safeguards and procedures under the CrPC are available to the accused. It delineates the powers of the Special Court and ensures that the principles of natural justice and fair trial are upheld in PMLA proceedings.

➤ Relevant Precedents and Citations Used

1. State of Kerala v. Kandath Distilleries (2013): Discussed the discretionary nature of certain statutory powers.

2. National Insurance Company Ltd vs. Boghara Polyfab Pvt. Ltd (2009): Addressed the court's ability to go into the question of liability even after the issuance of a full and final discharge voucher.

➤ Practical Implications on Advocates and Judges

For advocates, this judgment provides a clearer framework for defending clients in PMLA cases, ensuring they can leverage CrPC provisions effectively. For judges, it sets a precedent on how to integrate CrPC procedures in PMLA cases, especially regarding bail and the definition of custody.

➤ Conclusion

The judgment reinforces the applicability of CrPC provisions to PMLA proceedings, ensuring that accused individuals are afforded the procedural protections available under the CrPC. This alignment promotes a more just and fair judicial process, balancing the stringent requirements of the PMLA with the procedural safeguards of the CrPC.

Scan Me to Download

Case-19

"VICTIM'S VOICE UPHOLDING CONVICTIONS IN THE GANG RAPE CASE

SELVAMANI VERSUS THE STATE REP. BY THE INSPECTOR OF POLICE

> **Background of the Case**

The case pertains to an appeal challenging the final judgment and order dated 27th August 2019, passed by the learned Single Judge of the High Court of Judicature at Madras. The High Court dismissed Criminal Appeal Nos. 449 and 840 of 2012. The appellant, Accused No. 2, along with Accused Nos. 3 and 4, filed Criminal Appeal No. 840 of 2012 under Section 374 of the Criminal Procedure Code, 1973, challenging the judgment and order dated 26th June 2012 passed by the learned Additional District and Sessions Judge, Court No. III, Thirupathur, Vellore District, in Sessions Case No. 277 of 2010. The trial court had convicted and sentenced the accused for offences under Section 376(2)(g) and 506(1) of the Indian Penal Code, 1860, and Section 4 of the Tamil Nadu Prevention of Women Harassment Act.

➤ Facts

1. Incident Report: On 28th January 2006, the victim (PW-1) reported to Police Station Vaniyampadi Town that she had been gang-raped.

2. FIR Registration: An FIR was registered under Sections 341, 323, 376, and 506(2) IPC, along with Section 4 of the Tamil Nadu Prevention of Women Harassment Act.

3. Investigation: The Inspector of Police, Loganthan (PW-13), investigated the scene, recorded statements, and arrested the accused.

4. Victim's Statement: The victim's statement under Section 164 CrPC was recorded by the Judicial Magistrate, Thirupattur.

5. Prosecution's Case: The victim was working at Emerald Shoe Company. On 27th January 2006, around 7 PM, the manager (Accused No. 1) took her to a secluded place where other accused persons were present. They threatened her, stripped her, and gang-raped her until 3:30 AM. She escaped and reported the incident to her mother (PW-2) and aunt (PW-3).

6. Trial: The trial court framed charges under Sections 376(2)(g) and 506(1) IPC and Section 4 of the Tamil Nadu Prevention of Women Harassment Act. The accused pleaded not guilty. The prosecution examined 14 witnesses and presented 25 exhibits.

> **Issues**

1. Credibility of Witnesses: The main issue revolved around whether the testimonies of the victim and other witnesses could be trusted, especially given their inconsistencies during cross-examination.

2. Medical Evidence: The alignment of medical evidence with the victim's account.

3. Legal Standards for Conviction: The appropriate legal standards and precedents for convicting the accused based on available evidence.

> **Important Points Considered in the Judgment**

1. Testimonies of Victim and Witnesses: The trial and High Court both heavily relied on the testimonies of the victim, her mother (PW-2), and her aunt (PW-3).

2. Medical Evidence: The medical examination supported the victim's account, showing injuries consistent with forcible sexual intercourse.

3. Hostile Witnesses: The impact of the prosecution witnesses turning hostile during cross-examination.

4. Precedents: Various precedents regarding the handling of hostile witnesses and the reliance on their testimonies were considered.

➤ Legal Issues Involved

1. Evidentiary Value of Hostile Witnesses: The legal principle regarding the reliance on testimonies of witnesses who turn hostile.

2. Consistency and Corroboration: The requirement of consistency and corroboration between the victim's testimony and other evidence.

3. Conviction Standards: The standards required to uphold a conviction in rape cases, especially gang rape.

➤ Court's Decision and Reasoning

The court upheld the conviction and dismissed the appeal. The court reasoned that:

1. Consistency in Initial Statements: Despite turning hostile during cross-examination, the initial statements of the victim and her relatives (PW-2 and PW-3) were consistent and corroborated by medical evidence.

2. Hostile Witness Doctrine: The court cited several precedents to argue that the testimony of a hostile witness is not entirely discarded but is considered for its reliable parts.

3. Corroborative Evidence: The medical evidence provided strong corroboration for the victim's account, establishing the occurrence of rape.

➤ Importance and Impact of the Judgment

1. Reinforcement of Legal Principles: The judgment reinforced the legal principles regarding the treatment of hostile witnesses and the standards for corroborating evidence in rape cases.

2. Emphasis on Victim's Testimony: The decision underscored the importance of the victim's testimony and its corroboration through other evidence.

3. Judicial Approach: The judgment illustrated the judiciary's approach to handling serious crimes like rape and ensuring justice is served despite challenges in witness testimony.

➤ Relevant Precedents and Citations Used

1. Khujji @ Surendra Tiwari v. State of Madhya Pradesh (1991) 3 SCC 627: On the evidentiary value of hostile witnesses.

2. C. Muniappan and Others v. State of Tamil Nadu (2010) 9 SCC 567: Reiterated principles regarding hostile witnesses and corroboration.

3. Vinod Kumar v. State of Punjab (2015) 3 SCC 220: Emphasized the timely cross-examination of witnesses to avoid undue influence.

➢ Practical Implications on Advocates and Judges

1. Handling Hostile Witnesses: Advocates and judges must be adept at dealing with hostile witnesses and discerning the credible parts of their testimonies.

2. Cross-Examination Timing: The case highlights the need for prompt cross-examination to prevent witness tampering.

3. Victim's Testimony Weight: It emphasizes the substantial weight given to a victim's testimony when corroborated by other evidence.

➢ Conclusion

The case demonstrates the complexities involved in rape trials, particularly concerning witness credibility and the corroborative value of medical evidence. The judgment reinforces the judicial commitment to upholding convictions in serious crimes like gang rape, relying on a holistic evaluation of evidence despite challenges posed by hostile witnesses. This case serves as a significant precedent for future cases involving similar legal and factual matrices.

Scan Me to Download

Case-20

QUASHED! HOW SETTLEMENT ENDED THE LOAN FRAUD SAGA

K. BHARTHI DEVI AND ANR. VERSUS STATE OF TELANGANA & ANR.

> Background of the Case:

In K. Bharthi Devi and Anr. v. State of Telangana & Anr., the appellants were accused in a case involving fraudulent loan transactions with the Indian Bank. The firm M/s Sirish Traders, owned by the first accused, K. Suresh Kumar, took a loan from Indian Bank, Osmanganj Branch, Hyderabad. The appellants, wives of accused Nos. 1 and 2, were alleged to have acted as guarantors for this loan. When the loan turned into a Non-Performing Asset (NPA), it was discovered that the collateral documents submitted by the accused were fake and forged. A complaint was lodged, and the CBI's Economic Offence Wing (EOW) initiated an investigation.

The appellants sought to quash the charge-sheet against them, citing that a One Time Settlement (OTS) had been reached between the bank and the accused, and the loan was settled. Despite this, the High Court of Hyderabad refused to quash the charges, stating that the use of fraudulent documents was a crime against society.

➤ Facts:

1. M/s Sirish Traders, owned by K. Suresh Kumar, took loans secured by collateral documents allegedly executed by the accused.

2. The loans turned into NPAs by March 31, 2010, and the bank initiated proceedings before the Debts Recovery Tribunal (DRT).

3. During DRT proceedings, the bank found that the title documents used to secure the loan were fake and lodged a complaint.

4. The CBI filed a charge sheet, accusing the appellants under IPC Sections 120-B, 420, 409, 467, 468, and 471, and under Sections 13(1)(d) and 13(2) of the Prevention of Corruption Act.

5. The accused paid Rs. 3.8 crores under a One Time Settlement (OTS), and the bank issued a No Dues Certificate.

6. The appellants argued that the settlement resolved the matter and sought quashing of the criminal charges.

➤ Legal Issues:

1. Can criminal proceedings be quashed after a private settlement between the bank and the accused?

2. Do non-compoundable offences like forgery still warrant prosecution despite settlement in civil matters?

3. Whether continuing the trial after a civil settlement would amount to an abuse of the legal process.

➤ Court's Decision and Reasoning:

The Supreme Court quashed the criminal proceedings against the appellants. It held:

1. Predominant Civil Nature of the Dispute: The dispute was primarily financial, involving loan recovery, which had been settled.

2. Overriding Importance of Settlement: Given the settlement and the bank's acceptance of the OTS, the continuance of criminal proceedings would be an exercise in futility.

3. Appellants' Minor Role: The court noted that the appellants were wives of the main accused and had no significant role in the fraudulent activities.

4. Precedents Supporting Quashing: The Court cited several precedents (like Nikhil Merchant v. CBI and Gian Singh v. State of Punjab) where criminal cases with civil disputes were quashed after settlements.

➤ Relevant Precedents:

- ✓ CBI v. Duncans Agro Industries Ltd.: Similar to the present case, where the court quashed criminal proceedings as the civil dispute had been resolved.

- ✓ Nikhil Merchant v. CBI: The Court quashed criminal charges even in non-compoundable offences due to a civil settlement.

- ✓ Gian Singh v. State of Punjab: Established that criminal proceedings can be quashed even for non-compoundable offences when the dispute is overwhelmingly civil in nature.

> Importance and Impact of the Judgement:

This judgment emphasizes that in cases involving financial disputes or civil wrongs, especially when settlements are reached, criminal prosecution may not always serve justice. It highlights the court's approach in distinguishing between crimes that are purely private disputes and those that affect society at large.

> Practical Implications for Advocates and Judges:

1. Advocates: Can rely on this judgment to argue for quashing criminal proceedings when civil disputes are settled, especially in financial and commercial transactions.

2. Judges: The judgment reinforces the importance of considering the broader impact of criminal prosecutions and balancing the scales between punishment and the resolution of private disputes.

Conclusion:

The Supreme Court upheld the principle that where civil disputes with some criminal overtones are settled amicably, the continuation of criminal proceedings may be an abuse of the judicial process. This case serves as a significant reference point for future matters where financial disputes spill over into criminal law, underlining the court's power to quash such proceedings in the interest of justice.

Scan Me to Download

******

www.ingramcontent.com/pod-product-compliance
Lightning Source LLC
Chambersburg PA
CBHW071100240526
45471CB00016B/2216